TRIBE ACTION PLAN WORKBOOK
HOW TO BUILD INFECTIOUS MEMBERSHIP COMMUNITIES WITH YOUR BRAND

THE PURPOSE OF THIS WORKBOOK

Dear Fearless CEO,

In my career it was never enough to speak about what you are going to do, instead it was absolutely important to show results. This is also something that I have carried over in my entrepreneurial journey as well. The purpose of this work book is to help you do two things: TAKE ACTION and SEE RESULTS.

We accomplish this by focusing on 4 key areas for the next 120 days.

- Plan
- Build
- Implement
- Evaluate

Each month will be dedicated to a key area and you will have the opportunity to strategize, create action items, anchor them to dates, and capture your thoughts on your efforts!

As we navigate through each month and each key area, you will have guidance along the way on how to fill out each section! You are not alone, you have read the book, you received the nuggets of info and now it's time for you to do the work and guess what? YOU GOT THIS!!!

Let's Get to Work!

Nicole E. xoxo, Doss

MONTH 1
PLAN PHASE

Write the vision and make it plain

PLAN PHASE MONTH_____

In this plan phase it is your job to get crystal clear on what you are going to build for your tribe. I want you to think about it first as a brain storm and then I want you to start narrowing it down! Let's get to work!

THE BRAINSTORM

In the book TRIBE we discussed the different ways you can build a tribal business model for your brand, in the space below capture all of the ways you could possibly create a community for your tribe based off the core values, mission, and vision of your business.

THE SKINNY

You captured really great ideas in the space above. Now I want you to skinny the list down to 1 way you would absolutely LOVE to start a community for your brand! In the space below use the blank space as a canvas to creatively map out what this vision is. What is the community, how will it engage your tribe, what will the value be, and how will you charge for this community!

CEO CORNER

In this section, capture how building this tribal business model makes you feel. Why? Your answers will show you how you will go about making this happen. Are you nervous, doubtful, excited, or overwhelmed? No worries, capture how you feel but more importantly, write down how your feelings are going to drive your next action. If you find that your feelings are not positive, go back to the brain storm and see what other options are open for your business. If they are positive let's capture what's next for you!

30 DAY

Now that you know what you want to create ,plan out what needs to be done in order to take this from conception to reality

SUN	MON	TUES	WED

ACTION PLANNER

Map out your month and clear obstacles to make way for your vision.

THURS	FRI	SAT

DAILY PLANNER

Now map out your week!

MONDAY

☐ CHECK ONCE TASKS ARE COMPLETE

TUESDAY

☐ CHECK ONCE TASKS ARE COMPLETE

WEDNESDAY

☐ CHECK ONCE TASKS ARE COMPLETE

DAILY PLANNER

Being intentional is going to help you see desired results

THURSDAY

☐ CHECK ONCE TASKS ARE COMPLETE

FRIDAY

☐ CHECK ONCE TASKS ARE COMPLETE

SAT/SUN

☐ CHECK ONCE TASKS ARE COMPLETE

DAILY PLANNER

Now map out your week!

MONDAY

CHECK ONCE TASKS ARE COMPLETE

TUESDAY

CHECK ONCE TASKS ARE COMPLETE

WEDNESDAY

CHECK ONCE TASKS ARE COMPLETE

DAILY PLANNER

Being intentional is going to help you see desired results

THURSDAY

CHECK ONCE TASKS ARE COMPLETE

FRIDAY

CHECK ONCE TASKS ARE COMPLETE

SAT/SUN

CHECK ONCE TASKS ARE COMPLETE

DAILY PLANNER

Now map out your week!

MONDAY

☐ CHECK ONCE TASKS ARE COMPLETE

TUESDAY

☐ CHECK ONCE TASKS ARE COMPLETE

WEDNESDAY

☐ CHECK ONCE TASKS ARE COMPLETE

DAILY PLANNER

Being intentional is going to help you see desired results

THURSDAY

☐   CHECK ONCE TASKS ARE COMPLETE

FRIDAY

☐   CHECK ONCE TASKS ARE COMPLETE

SAT/SUN

☐   CHECK ONCE TASKS ARE COMPLETE

DAILY PLANNER

Now map out your week!

MONDAY

☐ CHECK ONCE TASKS ARE COMPLETE

TUESDAY

☐ CHECK ONCE TASKS ARE COMPLETE

WEDNESDAY

☐ CHECK ONCE TASKS ARE COMPLETE

DAILY PLANNER

Being intentional is going to help you see desired results

THURSDAY

☐ CHECK ONCE TASKS ARE COMPLETE

FRIDAY

☐ CHECK ONCE TASKS ARE COMPLETE

SAT/SUN

☐ CHECK ONCE TASKS ARE COMPLETE

DAILY PLANNER

Now map out your week!

MONDAY

☐ CHECK ONCE TASKS ARE COMPLETE

TUESDAY

☐ CHECK ONCE TASKS ARE COMPLETE

WEDNESDAY

☐ CHECK ONCE TASKS ARE COMPLETE

DAILY PLANNER

Being intentional is going to help you see desired results

THURSDAY

☐ CHECK ONCE TASKS ARE COMPLETE

FRIDAY

☐ CHECK ONCE TASKS ARE COMPLETE

SAT/SUN

☐ CHECK ONCE TASKS ARE COMPLETE

DAILY PLANNER

Now map out your week!

MONDAY

☐ CHECK ONCE TASKS ARE COMPLETE

TUESDAY

☐ CHECK ONCE TASKS ARE COMPLETE

WEDNESDAY

☐ CHECK ONCE TASKS ARE COMPLETE

DAILY PLANNER

Being intentional is going to help you see desired results

THURSDAY

☐　　CHECK ONCE TASKS ARE COMPLETE

FRIDAY

☐　　CHECK ONCE TASKS ARE COMPLETE

SAT/SUN

☐　　CHECK ONCE TASKS ARE COMPLETE

JOURNAL IT BO$$

Reflection is going to help you kill it in the coming months! Reflect on your efforts, ah-ha moments and business lessons!

_____

_____

_____

_____

_____

_____

_____

_____

_____

_____

_____

_____

_____

_____

_____

_____

MONTH 2
BUILD PHASE
Build the Foundation of What You Dream

BUILD PHASE MONTH_____

Let's start putting some structure around your vision with the 4 W's!

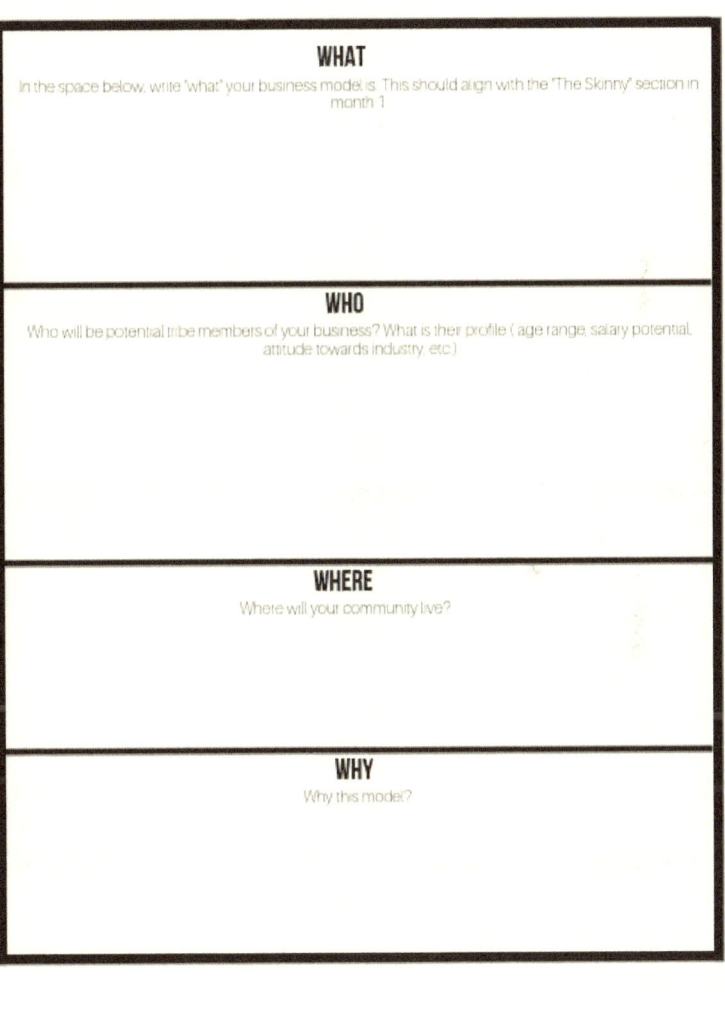

WHAT

In the space below, write 'what' your business model is. This should align with the 'The Skinny' section in month 1

WHO

Who will be potential tribe members of your business? What is their profile (age range, salary potential, attitude towards industry, etc.)

WHERE

Where will your community live?

WHY

Why this model?

S.W.O.T

You are going to identify the Strengths, Weaknesses, Opportunities, and Threats of your tribal business model.

STRENGTH
List the strengths of this model you are building. What are the Pros?

WEAKNESS
What are some areas that may be considered a weakness regarding the building of your model?

TIME

Read each section and fill it out accordingly. Keep in mind that Strength and Weakness are focused on internal factors and Opportunities and Threats are focused on external factors.

OPPORTUNITIES
What opportunities exist in your industry that makes this community a viable idea?

THREATS
What is happening in your industry that may work against this idea?

BUILDERS CORNER

This is your time to build your tribal business model. In the space below capture what you resources you will need to make it happen. Capture if there are costs involved, platforms you need to create, websites etc.

Don't leave anything on the table. Make sure you capture it all!

30 DAY

You know what it takes to build your tribal business model!

SUN	MON	TUES	WED

ACTION PLANNER

Now you have to anchor your tasks to dates!

THURS	FRI	SAT

DAILY PLANNER

Each week you should have action items

MONDAY

☐ CHECK ONCE TASKS ARE COMPLETE

TUESDAY

☐ CHECK ONCE TASKS ARE COMPLETE

WEDNESDAY

☐ CHECK ONCE TASKS ARE COMPLETE

DAILY PLANNER

created for you to be able to build your tribal business model!

THURSDAY

☐ CHECK ONCE TASKS ARE COMPLETE

FRIDAY

☐ CHECK ONCE TASKS ARE COMPLETE

SAT/SUN

☐ CHECK ONCE TASKS ARE COMPLETE

DAILY PLANNER

MONDAY

CHECK ONCE TASKS ARE COMPLETE

TUESDAY

CHECK ONCE TASKS ARE COMPLETE

WEDNESDAY

CHECK ONCE TASKS ARE COMPLETE

DAILY PLANNER

Being intentional is going to help you see desired results

THURSDAY

☐ CHECK ONCE TASKS ARE COMPLETE

FRIDAY

☐ CHECK ONCE TASKS ARE COMPLETE

SAT/SUN

☐ CHECK ONCE TASKS ARE COMPLETE

DAILY PLANNER

You have a fire in your belly to get this thing going. Let's kill it this week!

MONDAY

☐   CHECK ONCE TASKS ARE COMPLETE

TUESDAY

☐   CHECK ONCE TASKS ARE COMPLETE

WEDNESDAY

☐   CHECK ONCE TASKS ARE COMPLETE

DAILY PLANNER

THURSDAY

☐ CHECK ONCE TASKS ARE COMPLETE

FRIDAY

☐ CHECK ONCE TASKS ARE COMPLETE

SAT/SUN

☐ CHECK ONCE TASKS ARE COMPLETE

DAILY PLANNER

You will have to set your intentions each week.

MONDAY

☐ CHECK ONCE TASKS ARE COMPLETE

TUESDAY

☐ CHECK ONCE TASKS ARE COMPLETE

WEDNESDAY

☐ CHECK ONCE TASKS ARE COMPLETE

DAILY PLANNER

Use the white space to capture notes and write your intentions for this week.

THURSDAY

☐ CHECK ONCE TASKS ARE COMPLETE

FRIDAY

☐ CHECK ONCE TASKS ARE COMPLETE

SAT/SUN

☐ CHECK ONCE TASKS ARE COMPLETE

DAILY PLANNER

This month is going to wrap up soon.

MONDAY

☐   CHECK ONCE TASKS ARE COMPLETE

TUESDAY

☐   CHECK ONCE TASKS ARE COMPLETE

WEDNESDAY

☐   CHECK ONCE TASKS ARE COMPLETE

DAILY PLANNER

Create some kick-ass goals in there. You got this!

THURSDAY

CHECK ONCE TASKS ARE COMPLETE

FRIDAY

CHECK ONCE TASKS ARE COMPLETE

SAT/SUN

CHECK ONCE TASKS ARE COMPLETE

DAILY PLANNER

This month is going to wrap up soon.

MONDAY

☐ CHECK ONCE TASKS ARE COMPLETE

TUESDAY

☐ CHECK ONCE TASKS ARE COMPLETE

WEDNESDAY

☐ CHECK ONCE TASKS ARE COMPLETE

DAILY PLANNER

Create some kick-ass goals in there. You got this!

THURSDAY

CHECK ONCE TASKS ARE COMPLETE

FRIDAY

CHECK ONCE TASKS ARE COMPLETE

SAT/SUN

CHECK ONCE TASKS ARE COMPLETE

JOURNAL IT BO$$

You are building a community that is going to bless others... what worked this month? What needs to be reconsidered? Capture your thoughts.

_____

_____

_____

_____

_____

_____

_____

_____

_____

_____

_____

_____

_____

_____

_____

_____

_____

MONTH 3
IMPLEMENT PHASE

There is No Time Like the Present to Put
Your Thoughts into Action!

IMPLEMENT PHASE MONTH_____

Map Out Your Implementation Phase

WHAT HAVE YOU BUILT?

WHAT PLATFORM ARE YOU USING FOR YOUR TRIBE?

WHAT MESSAGING WILL YOU BE USING TO COMMUNICATE TO YOUR AUDIENCE?

WHEN IS YOUR MARKETING CAMPAIGN GOING TO BEGIN?

WILL IT INCLUDE A FREEBIE WITH THE UP-SELL BEING YOUR TRIBAL MODEL?

HAVE YOU MAPPED OUT YOUR COMMUNICATION PLAN?

HAVE YOU CREATED THE MARKETING MATERIALS?

DO YOU HAVE EXISTING POTENTIAL TRIBE MEMBERS IN YOUR PIPELINE?

HAVE YOU CREATED SOCIAL MEDIA ADS TO SPREAD THE WORD?

WHAT OTHER BRANDS CAN YOU REACH OUT TO FOR MARKETING AND SPREADING THE
WORD (IE. AMBASSADORS, PODCASTS, WRITE-UPS ETC.)

MARKETING PLAN

PRODUCT This is the service or product you are providing. This will be your Tribal business model.

PRICE This should be aligned to the perceived and real value of the product

MARKETING PLAN

BUILD YOUR MARKETING PLAN USING THE 4 P'S OF MARKETING

PROMOTION This is the public relation efforts where you communicate why consumers need your product and why it is of value.

PLACEMENT How you will get your product in front of your potential tribe members.

30 DAY

Your JOB is to LAUNCH Your Tribe this Month!

SUN	MON	TUES	WED

ACTION PLANNER

But there are steps to get you there. Map Out Your Actions

THURS	FRI	SAT

DAILY PLANNER

You have to launch this month but is your communications, marketing,

MONDAY

☐ CHECK ONCE TASKS ARE COMPLETE

TUESDAY

☐ CHECK ONCE TASKS ARE COMPLETE

WEDNESDAY

☐ CHECK ONCE TASKS ARE COMPLETE

DAILY PLANNER

and sales efforts planned? If not use your daily planner section action items mapped out!

THURSDAY

☐ CHECK ONCE TASKS ARE COMPLETE

FRIDAY

☐ CHECK ONCE TASKS ARE COMPLETE

SAT/SUN

☐ CHECK ONCE TASKS ARE COMPLETE

DAILY PLANNER

Are you excited about your launch? I am so let's get you closer to this reality!

MONDAY

☐ CHECK ONCE TASKS ARE COMPLETE

TUESDAY

☐ CHECK ONCE TASKS ARE COMPLETE

WEDNESDAY

☐ CHECK ONCE TASKS ARE COMPLETE

DAILY PLANNER

Being intentional is going to help you see desired results !

THURSDAY

☐ CHECK ONCE TASKS ARE COMPLETE

FRIDAY

☐ CHECK ONCE TASKS ARE COMPLETE

SAT/SUN

☐ CHECK ONCE TASKS ARE COMPLETE

DAILY PLANNER

Soft launch or hard launch, that's really the question!

MONDAY

| | CHECK ONCE TASKS ARE COMPLETE |

TUESDAY

| | CHECK ONCE TASKS ARE COMPLETE |

WEDNESDAY

| | CHECK ONCE TASKS ARE COMPLETE |

DAILY PLANNER

Just decide how much of a buzz you want to generate!

THURSDAY

☐ CHECK ONCE TASKS ARE COMPLETE

FRIDAY

☐ CHECK ONCE TASKS ARE COMPLETE

SAT/SUN

☐ CHECK ONCE TASKS ARE COMPLETE

DAILY PLANNER

You will have to set your intentions each week.

MONDAY

☐ CHECK ONCE TASKS ARE COMPLETE

TUESDAY

☐ CHECK ONCE TASKS ARE COMPLETE

WEDNESDAY

☐ CHECK ONCE TASKS ARE COMPLETE

DAILY PLANNER

Doing so will help you accomplish your goals!

THURSDAY

☐ CHECK ONCE TASKS ARE COMPLETE

FRIDAY

☐ CHECK ONCE TASKS ARE COMPLETE

SAT/SUN

☐ CHECK ONCE TASKS ARE COMPLETE

DAILY PLANNER

This month is going to wrap up soon.

MONDAY

☐   CHECK ONCE TASKS ARE COMPLETE

TUESDAY

☐   CHECK ONCE TASKS ARE COMPLETE

WEDNESDAY

☐   CHECK ONCE TASKS ARE COMPLETE

DAILY PLANNER

Create some kick-ass goals in there. You got this!

THURSDAY

☐ CHECK ONCE TASKS ARE COMPLETE

FRIDAY

☐ CHECK ONCE TASKS ARE COMPLETE

SAT/SUN

☐ CHECK ONCE TASKS ARE COMPLETE

DAILY PLANNER

This month is going to wrap up soon.

MONDAY

☐ CHECK ONCE TASKS ARE COMPLETE

TUESDAY

☐ CHECK ONCE TASKS ARE COMPLETE

WEDNESDAY

☐ CHECK ONCE TASKS ARE COMPLETE

DAILY PLANNER

Create some kick-ass goals in there. You got this!

THURSDAY

☐ CHECK ONCE TASKS ARE COMPLETE

FRIDAY

☐ CHECK ONCE TASKS ARE COMPLETE

SAT/SUN

☐ CHECK ONCE TASKS ARE COMPLETE

JOURNAL IT BO$$

You did it!!!!!! Or did you? Either way there are some awesome ah-ha moments and lessons to
learn from and milestones to celebrate. Capture it all here!

_____

_____

_____

_____

_____

_____

_____

_____

_____

_____

_____

_____

_____

_____

_____

MONTH 4
EVALUATION PHASE

Putting something out there is not enough.
You have to reflect , tweak, and put it back
out there.

EVALUATION PHASE

.

In the past three months, you have done tremendous work on building your tribal business model. But now it is time for you to identify what is working and what's not working during this evaluation phase. We are going to explore both internal and external factors that can impact the viable sustainability of your tribal business model. Once we identify things that are working out wonderfully for you those are the things that you will continue to do, the things that need to be revamped, we will tweak those things so they work better moving forward!

Don't get discouraged if things need to be reworked. That's literally what happens when businesses introduce something new to the market. This is why the evaluation phase is so important.

So let's start evaluating now!

EVALUATION PHASE

In the space below, read each box and write the answer. This will allow you to analyze your efforts!

THIS RIGHT HERE... SOOOO WORKED!

What worked for you when you implemented your tribal business model last month?

I WENT FULL FORCE BUT... IT JUST DIDN'T WORK THE WAY I EXPECTED IT TO.

Now let's talk about what didn't work so well.

MONTH_____

Don't over think it, you can use some of the moments you capture in the past three months in the "Journal" section of the work book.

WHAT NEEDS TO BE REMOVED

Often times when we introduce something new in our business, we find that there are somethings that sounded great in theory but aren't that great in reality.

WHAT WOULD YOU LIKE TO ADD

Is there something missing from the equation? What would you like to add?

30 DAY

You have identified some things that you would like to start, stop, or continue.

SUN	MON	TUES	WED

ACTION PLANNER

Tak a moment and add those items to your planner!

THURS	FRI	SAT

DAILY PLANNER

Now map out your week!

MONDAY

☐ CHECK ONCE TASKS ARE COMPLETE

TUESDAY

☐ CHECK ONCE TASKS ARE COMPLETE

WEDNESDAY

☐ CHECK ONCE TASKS ARE COMPLETE

DAILY PLANNER

Being intentional is going to help you see desired results

THURSDAY

☐ CHECK ONCE TASKS ARE COMPLETE

FRIDAY

☐ CHECK ONCE TASKS ARE COMPLETE

SAT/SUN

☐ CHECK ONCE TASKS ARE COMPLETE

DAILY PLANNER

Now map out your week!

MONDAY

☐ CHECK ONCE TASKS ARE COMPLETE

TUESDAY

☐ CHECK ONCE TASKS ARE COMPLETE

WEDNESDAY

☐ CHECK ONCE TASKS ARE COMPLETE

DAILY PLANNER

Being intentional is going to help you see desired results

THURSDAY

☐ CHECK ONCE TASKS ARE COMPLETE

FRIDAY

☐ CHECK ONCE TASKS ARE COMPLETE

SAT/SUN

☐ CHECK ONCE TASKS ARE COMPLETE

DAILY PLANNER

Now map out your week!

MONDAY

☐ CHECK ONCE TASKS ARE COMPLETE

TUESDAY

☐ CHECK ONCE TASKS ARE COMPLETE

WEDNESDAY

☐ CHECK ONCE TASKS ARE COMPLETE

DAILY PLANNER

Being intentional is going to help you see desired results

THURSDAY

☐ CHECK ONCE TASKS ARE COMPLETE

FRIDAY

☐ CHECK ONCE TASKS ARE COMPLETE

SAT/SUN

☐ CHECK ONCE TASKS ARE COMPLETE

DAILY PLANNER

Now map out your week!

MONDAY

CHECK ONCE TASKS ARE COMPLETE

TUESDAY

CHECK ONCE TASKS ARE COMPLETE

WEDNESDAY

CHECK ONCE TASKS ARE COMPLETE

DAILY PLANNER

Being intentional is going to help you see desired results

THURSDAY

CHECK ONCE TASKS ARE COMPLETE

FRIDAY

CHECK ONCE TASKS ARE COMPLETE

SAT/SUN

CHECK ONCE TASKS ARE COMPLETE

DAILY PLANNER

Now map out your week!

MONDAY

☐ CHECK ONCE TASKS ARE COMPLETE

TUESDAY

☐ CHECK ONCE TASKS ARE COMPLETE

WEDNESDAY

☐ CHECK ONCE TASKS ARE COMPLETE

DAILY PLANNER

Being intentional is going to help you see desired results

THURSDAY

☐ CHECK ONCE TASKS ARE COMPLETE

FRIDAY

☐ CHECK ONCE TASKS ARE COMPLETE

SAT/SUN

☐ CHECK ONCE TASKS ARE COMPLETE

DAILY PLANNER

Now map out your week!

MONDAY

CHECK ONCE TASKS ARE COMPLETE

TUESDAY

CHECK ONCE TASKS ARE COMPLETE

WEDNESDAY

CHECK ONCE TASKS ARE COMPLETE

DAILY PLANNER

Being intentional is going to help you see desired results

THURSDAY

☐ CHECK ONCE TASKS ARE COMPLETE

FRIDAY

☐ CHECK ONCE TASKS ARE COMPLETE

SAT/SUN

☐ CHECK ONCE TASKS ARE COMPLETE

JOURNAL IT BO$$

Reflection is going to help you kill it in the coming months! Reflect on your efforts, ah-ha moments and business lessons!

_____

_____

_____

_____

_____

_____

_____

_____

_____

_____

_____

_____

_____

_____

_____